BUILDING BY DESIGN

ENGINEERING
BURJ KHALIFA

BY CECILIA PINTO McCARTHY

CONTENT CONSULTANT
Tracy Kijewski-Correa
Associate Professor, College of Engineering
University of Notre Dame

Core Library

An Imprint of Abdo Publishing
abdopublishing.com

Cover image: Burj Khalifa rises high above Dubai, in
the United Arab Emirates (UAE).

abdopublishing.com

Published by Abdo Publishing, a division of ABDO, PO Box 398166,
Minneapolis, Minnesota 55439. Copyright © 2018 by Abdo Consulting
Group, Inc. International copyrights reserved in all countries. No part of this
book may be reproduced in any form without written permission from the
publisher. Core Library™ is a trademark and logo of Abdo Publishing.

Printed in the United States of America, North Mankato, Minnesota
082017
012018

Cover Photo: Shutterstock Images
Interior Photos: Shutterstock Images, 1; Mohammed Tareq/iStockphoto, 4–5, 43; View Pictures/
Universal Images Group/Getty Images, 6; Dave Newman/Shutterstock Images, 9; Chris Jackson/
Getty Images Entertainment/Getty Images, 12–13; iStockphoto, 15; Kamran Jebreili/AP Images,
17, 25, 28; Red Line Editorial, 20; Victor Romero/AP Images, 22–23, 45; Chris Jackson/Getty
Images News/Getty Images, 27; Umar Shariff/Shutterstock Images, 30; James D. Morgan/Rex/AP
Images, 32–33; Anton Gvozdikov/Shutterstock Images, 34; Imre Solt/Barcroft Media/Getty Images,
36; Alisdair Miller/Solent News/Rex/AP Images, 38–39

Editor: Arnold Ringstad
Imprint Designer: Maggie Villaume
Series Design Direction: Laura Polzin

Publisher's Cataloging-in-Publication Data

Names: McCarthy, Cecilia Pinto, author.
Title: Engineering Burj Khalifa / by Cecilia Pinto McCarthy.
Description: Minneapolis, Minnesota : Abdo Publishing, 2018. | Series: Building by design |
    Includes online resources and index.
Identifiers: LCCN 2017946984 | ISBN 9781532113710 (lib.bdg.) | ISBN 9781532152597 (ebook)
Subjects: LCSH: Burj Khalifa (Dubai, United Arab Emirates)--Juvenile literature. | Building--
    Juvenile literature. | Skyscrapers--Juvenile literature. | Buildings--Juvenile literature.
Classification: DDC 720.483--dc23
LC record available at https://lccn.loc.gov/2017946984

CONTENTS

A RECORD SETTER

Burj Khalifa soars 2,717 feet (828 m) into the air. It rises above the desert city of Dubai, in the United Arab Emirates (UAE). The tower became the world's tallest when it was finished in 2009. It stands on a huge Y-shaped base. It spirals and tapers as it rises. The tower's shape mimics a local desert flower. Burj Khalifa's highest point is the tip of its steel spire.

The word *Burj* is Arabic for "tower." The building was originally called Burj Dubai. It was renamed to honor Sheikh Khalifa bin Zayed Al Nahyan. He is the president of the UAE.

Burj Khalifa towers over Dubai's other skyscrapers.

Large areas of grass and water are found at the tower's base.

In 2009, Dubai was close to financial disaster. Sheikh Khalifa loaned the city money. His loan prevented a crisis.

Burj Khalifa is a mega-skyscraper. This is a building more than 1,969 feet (600 m) tall. The tower is often called a vertical city. It includes 163 floors. They contain offices, apartments, and a hotel. The base of the tower stands within a green space called the Park. The Park features fountains and pools. Its trees and lush gardens create an oasis in the desert.

Burj Khalifa holds many records. It has the most floors of any tower. It also has the world's highest swimming pool and restaurant.

DOUBLE-DECK ELEVATORS

Fifty-seven elevators take people up and down in Burj Khalifa. Two of them are double-deck elevators. One elevator car is stacked atop another. They are the world's fastest double-deck elevators. They travel at 1,969 feet (600 m) per minute. Up to 28 passengers can ride them. The elevators go to an observation deck on the 124th floor. Inside the elevator, video screens showcase the tower and the city of Dubai.

A GLOBAL PARTNERSHIP

Burj Khalifa was the idea of Sheikh Mohammed bin Rashid Al Maktoum. Sheikh Mohammed is the ruler of

Dubai. He has worked to make Dubai a major world city. He believed a one-of-a-kind building would help in this mission.

Burj Khalifa was built through international cooperation. US architects and engineers worked with contractors from South Korea, Belgium, and the UAE. Burj Khalifa brings together art, science, and engineering. It symbolizes prosperity, ambition, and creativity.

A CHALLENGING PROJECT

The Chicago, Illinois, company Skidmore, Owings & Merrill (SOM) was hired to design Burj Khalifa. SOM is a leader in skyscraper design. It has built some of the world's tallest buildings. Its projects included two of Chicago's most famous skyscrapers. They are the John Hancock Center and Willis Tower. SOM architect Adrian Smith and structural engineer William F. Baker headed the design team. Burj Khalifa would be taller than any

SOM previously created the iconic Willis Tower in Chicago.

existing building. It would need to be beautiful and efficient. Above all, it would have to be safe.

Building Burj Khalifa would be difficult. The tower would be subject to fierce winds. It needed a secure foundation. But the desert ground is not solid. It is made up of sand and loose rock. Dubai's intense heat and sandstorms create harsh conditions. These issues did not stop Smith and Baker. They solved these problems with creative engineering solutions.

STRAIGHT TO THE
SOURCE

In the following passage, published before the tower took on its current name, architect Adrian Smith discusses how he developed the design:

> *In developing the initial concept for Burj Dubai, I searched for elements within the existing context and culture of the area to reflect on and draw inspiration from. Within the Middle East and in Dubai, there are strong influences of onion domes and pointed arches, and there are patterns that are indigenous to the region, some of which are flower-like with three elements, some with six and so on. . . . The form can be found in flower petals, leafs, seeds and animals such as birds, sea creatures. . . . The resulting impression is organic and plant like. . . . As the building rises from the ground it wants to feel like it is being sculpted from the earth and crystallized into a vertical stalactite of glass and steel.*

> Source: Adrian Smith. "Burj Dubai." *CTBUH*. CTBUH, 2008.
> Web. Accessed April 14, 2017.

What's the Big Idea?
Read the passage carefully. What inspired Adrian Smith's design for Burj Khalifa? What did Smith think about as he developed his design? Find two or three details in the passage that support the main idea.

THE DESIGN PROCESS

Before construction began, the SOM team developed a design. They applied math, science, and computer skills. Advanced computer software was used to plan the Burj's structure. The team calculated the amounts of concrete and steel needed. Engineers made 3-D models of the tower. The models would be used to test the Burj's stability. Building plans were changed many times during the design process.

PLANNING FOR FORCES

Creating extreme skyscrapers requires careful preparation. Forces push and pull on buildings.

Detailed models helped the design team plan the Burj Khalifa complex.

13

STRUCTURAL ENGINEERING

Structural engineering is a branch of civil engineering. Structural engineers analyze the forces that act on structures. They calculate pressures and stresses. They design buildings that withstand forces and stay stable. Engineers work with architects to construct buildings. Architects make sure buildings fit in with existing structures. Structural engineers check that structures meet safety standards.

Engineers call these forces loads. Natural factors also act on buildings. Wind and earthquakes are examples of these. Such forces can be unpredictable. They can cause severe damage.

Structural engineers plan for forces that act on a building. Gravity pulls buildings downward. The heavier the building, the greater the force of gravity on its foundation. Tall skyscrapers must rest on a solid foundation. This keeps buildings upright.

The tower's immense height and weight mean that extraordinary forces are acting upon it at all times.

The massive weight of the skyscraper itself creates compression and tension. Weight bends horizontal members, such as the floor slabs, through an action called flexure. This bending action causes compression. It shortens the upper part of the floor slab. At the same time, tension causes the bottom of the floor slab to stretch. Building materials must be strong to resist this compression and tension. Otherwise, these forces may damage a building. They could even cause it to collapse.

Fierce winds are a big problem for skyscrapers. Engineers knew that winds at the top of Burj Khalifa could reach 149 miles per hour (240 km/h). Wind blowing on a skyscraper causes swaying and twisting. Wind also causes the building to shear. In a building, shear forces cause parallel floor slabs to push or slide in opposite directions. This can cause the members that connect them, such as columns, to bend and break.

The unique shape of the Burj's foundation gives the tower stability and strength.

A UNIQUE DESIGN

Engineers made sure that Burj Khalifa would stand strong. A strong building begins with a secure foundation. Ideally, a building's foundation is attached to bedrock. But there is no bedrock under Dubai's desert. Engineers designed a different foundation to support the building's great weight.

Strong winds presented a difficult problem. Winds can make a building shake or even topple. Baker came up with a solution. He invented a new design. He called it the buttressed core. The base of Burj Khalifa is shaped like a Y. Baker ran strong concrete buttress walls down the middle of each wing of this Y shape. The three wings join at a six-sided concrete core. Each wing acts as a buttress, or support, for this central core. The three buttress wings stiffen the building and prevent it from twisting. They also help spread the weight of Burj Khalifa across a wider base. This helps keep the building steady.

CONFUSING THE WIND

Tall, slender buildings like Burj Khalifa are affected by vortex shedding. Wind hits the front of a skyscraper and flows around the building's sides. The wind separates as it goes around the building. This causes a difference of pressure to form on the front and back of the building. The pressure difference creates swirls of winds. The swirling winds are called vortices. They move away from, or are shed, from the building. When a building is the same shape all the way up, the vortices combine. They act together to push and pull at the building. This makes it sway. Skyscrapers are designed to move slightly from side to side. If skyscrapers are too stiff, they can be damaged by high winds. But buildings that sway too much are uncomfortable for people inside.

Engineers accounted for vortex

VORTEX
SHEDDING

The shape of Burj Khalifa changes as it gets taller. The lowest levels are the widest. The building narrows as it climbs higher. What happens as wind passes around Burj Khalifa at different levels? How does the building's changing shape affect wind patterns?

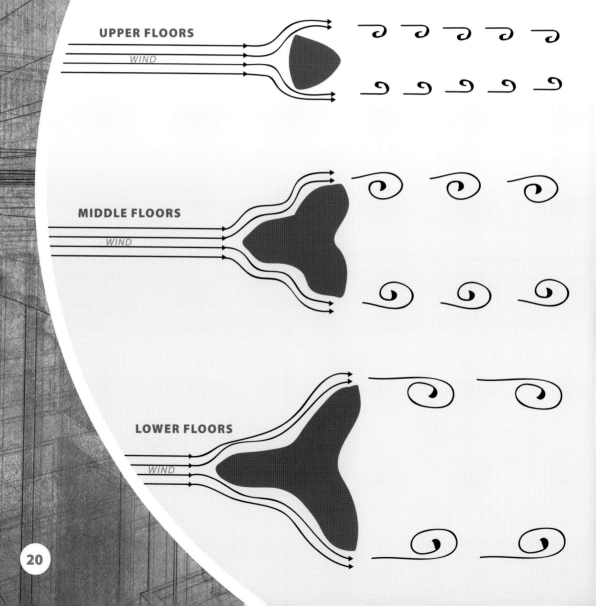

UPPER FLOORS

WIND

MIDDLE FLOORS

WIND

LOWER FLOORS

WIND

shedding in the shape of Burj Khalifa. They used techniques to prevent vortices from getting too strong. First, they created a six-sided design that resists twisting. Next, engineers made sure the Burj was not a uniform shape. As it climbs higher, the building changes shape. Every ten floors, the edges step inward. These setbacks make Burj Khalifa thinner as it spirals upward. This ensures that wind vortices cannot organize. The result is reduced wind force on the building.

FURTHER EVIDENCE

Chapter Two covers a lot of information about the planning and design of Burj Khalifa. What was one of the main points of this chapter? What evidence can you find to support this point? The website at the link below also discusses important factors that are considered before structures are constructed. Does the information support what you learned in the chapter? What new information did you learn from the website?

BUILDING SKYSCRAPERS

abdocorelibrary.com/engineering-burj-khalifa

BUILDING BURJ KHALIFA

Construction of Burj Khalifa was a difficult job. Work began in January 2004. The entire project spanned six years. Construction was completed in September 2009. At that time, the spire was finally added. The opening ceremony took place in January 2010. The completed structure used huge amounts of concrete, steel, and glass. The tower took 22 million person-hours to build. Its final cost was $1.5 billion.

A huge army of workers built Burj Khalifa.

THE SPIRE

Burj Khalifa is topped by a spire. It is made of 4,000 tons (3,629 metric tons) of steel. It was assembled inside the building. Then it was jacked up into position. Once it was placed, the spire was expanded to its full height. The spire is fitted with stainless steel fins. They match the spiral shapes of the rest of the building. The fins also help disrupt the wind flow. This reduces wind forces. The tip of the spire can be seen from up to 59 miles (95 km) away.

A SOUND FOUNDATION

The first step was to dig a foundation. Engineers chose friction pilings to anchor Burj Khalifa. Pile foundations use columns that go deep into the ground. They are used in areas where the soil is weak. Pile foundations can support tall, heavy buildings. They transfer the load of the building deep underground.

Burj Khalifa's foundation uses 192 friction pilings. Each piling is a long concrete cylinder five feet (1.5 m) in diameter. They transfer the load of the tower to the ground. The longer the pile, the more load it can

Engineers tour the site to see the foundation in 2005.

support. The pilings below Burj Khalifa extend 164 feet (50 m) deep. They are made of special concrete that resists water damage.

Above the pilings, workers poured the raft. The raft is the base of Burj Khalifa. It spreads the building's weight evenly onto the pilings. It is made of high-strength concrete 12 feet (3.7 m) thick. The foundation prevents Burj Khalifa from sinking into the sandy ground.

STEEL AND CONCRETE

After the foundation was set, workers began Burj Khalifa's superstructure. They used a construction method called jump forming. A steel-framed mold called formwork was made around the building's base. Next, steel reinforcement bars called rebar were put in the form. The bars added strength. Once the bars were set in place, concrete was poured into the form.

The tower stood 38 stories high by April 2006.

Burj Khalifa rose high above the rest of Dubai's skyline during construction.

The concrete hardened in 12 hours. Lifts then moved the framework up to the next level. The process was repeated. Burj Khalifa began to grow.

Working with concrete in a hot climate was a challenge. On a summer day, Dubai's temperature can climb to 113 degrees Fahrenheit (45°C). Workers needed a way to keep the concrete flowing. The heat could harden it too soon. A special concrete mixture was developed. It contained several chemicals. The chemicals kept the concrete fluid for a longer time. Concrete pumping was done at night. Ice was used to keep the concrete cool. This helped it flow easily.

As Burj Khalifa grew, workers needed a way to pump concrete higher. They used three of the world's most powerful concrete pumps. Over 32 months, they pumped more than 5.8 million cubic feet (165,000 cubic m) of concrete.

PROTECTIVE CLADDING

Once the lower floors were in place, workers began to install the tower's skin, called cladding. This covering does not support the skyscraper. Instead, it protects the building's interior from heat, wind, rain, and sand.

FLOOR
PLAN

Burj Khalifa is a mixed-use building. It contains a hotel, residences, and offices. Why do you think the floors are organized the way they are? Why do you think most hotel floors were put at a lower level than the apartments?

FLOOR NUMBER	USE
160–163	MECHANICAL
156–159	COMMUNICATION
155	MECHANICAL
149–154	OFFICES
148	OBSERVATION DECK
139–147	OFFICES
136–138	MECHANICAL
125–135	OFFICES
122–124	OBSERVATION DECKS AND CLUBS FOR APARTMENTS AND HOTEL
111–121	OFFICES
109–110	MECHANICAL
76–108	APARTMENTS
73–75	MECHANICAL
43–72	APARTMENTS
40–42	MECHANICAL
38–39	HOTEL
19–37	APARTMENTS
17–18	MECHANICAL
1–16	HOTEL

The Burj's cladding is made of steel and glass panels. Each panel weighs 800 pounds (363 kg). The glass contains two coatings. They reflect the sun's rays. Without the coatings, the temperature inside would become unbearably hot.

Covering Burj Khalifa with glass was a long process. Technicians raised the panels one at a time. They mounted them by hand. Installing the cladding began in May 2007. It ended in September 2009.

EXPLORE ONLINE

Chapter Three discusses how the jump form method was used to construct Burj Khalifa. The website below goes into more depth on this topic. How is the information from the website the same as the information in Chapter Three? What new information can you learn from the website?

JUMP FORM CONSTRUCTION
abdocorelibrary.com/engineering-burj-khalifa

CHAPTER
FOUR

BURJ KHALIFA TODAY

Burj Khalifa boasts 5.67 million square feet (530,000 sq m) of space. It has residences, offices, a hotel, lounges, shops, and fitness facilities. It also has four swimming pools. Two observation decks provide amazing views. The tower can hold up to 35,000 people. It operates like a small city. It has immense heating, cooling, and electrical demands. Building maintenance is a never-ending process.

The upper floors of the tower have enormous windows that offer incredible views.

An observation deck on the 125th floor provides stunning views of Dubai.

MECHANICAL, ELECTRICAL, AND PLUMBING SYSTEMS

Burj Khalifa's mechanical, electrical, and plumbing

(MEP) system is in its central core. Mechanical floors are

placed at every 30 stories. Each floor provides service

to the 15 floors above and below it. The MEP system is a vital part of the building. It helps maintain a comfortable environment.

All processes are controlled from a central computer room. Computer screens show everything going on in the building. From their seats, workers can see into elevator shafts. They can check wind speed. They can adjust air conditioning and pinpoint electrical problems.

Maintenance workers sit near part of the tower's lighting system.

Burj Khalifa's electrical substation is housed on the 155th floor. It is the world's highest substation. It delivers electrical power throughout the building. Electricity runs lighting, elevators, heating, and air conditioning systems.

STAYING SAFE

During planning, engineers were especially concerned with fire safety. Fire resistant materials were used in construction. Building protection systems include smoke sensors. All stairwells are surrounded by fireproof concrete. Exhaust systems clear the air of smoke and toxic gases. If a fire happens, automatic sprinklers go off. In case of emergency, a trained response team is ready to help. Every 25 floors, there are refuge areas. People can wait safely for help in these spaces.

Burj Khalifa's extreme height causes safety issues for aircraft. To prevent collisions, the Burj has high-intensity outdoor lights. The lights flash 40 times per minute, day and night.

A POPULAR ATTRACTION

Burj Khalifa has become a famous attraction. In 2013, more than 1.87 million visitors gazed out from the observation deck. Burj Khalifa regularly hosts special events, such as art and fashion shows. Each New

A photographer, along with maintenance workers, climbed to the tip of the spire in August 2011.

Year's Eve, people come to watch its spectacular

fireworks display.

Burj Khalifa is also a popular location for movie shoots and daredevil stunts. Part of the 2011 action movie *Mission Impossible: Ghost Protocol* was filmed

RECORD-BREAKING TOWERS

By 2020, Burj Khalifa was expected to lose its title as the world's tallest building. Another mega-skyscraper was scheduled to open that year. Jeddah Tower was planned to be built in Jeddah, Saudi Arabia. It would have 200 floors and be 3,280 feet (1,000 m) high. Burj Khalifa and Jeddah Tower share many similarities. Both buildings were designed by Adrian Smith. Like the Burj, Jeddah Tower's shape was inspired by desert plants.

at the tower. One scene features actor Tom Cruise. He leaps from a window. Then he scrambles across the Burj's glass panels. Several people have parachuted from the upper floors.

By 2017, designs were under way for buildings that would reach even higher. But Burj Khalifa remains an incredible achievement. This shimmering tower rises high above the desert city of Dubai. It shows the potential of state-of-the-art engineering and construction.

STRAIGHT TO THE
SOURCE

Traditional skyscrapers are built from concrete and steel. Here, writer Clay Risen describes a new building material called cross-laminated timber (CLT), which is made from layered wood:

From the outside, there is nothing flashy about the nine-story building called Stadthaus. . . . It's what's inside that makes Stadthaus stand out. Instead of steel and concrete, the floors, ceilings, elevator shafts, and stairwells are made entirely of wood. . . . The tower's strength and mass rely on a highly engineered material called cross-laminated timber (CLT). . . . Why the sudden interest in wood? Compared with steel or concrete, CLT . . . is cheaper, easier to assemble, and more fire resistant. . . . It's also more sustainable . . . the planet's urban citizenry will double in 36 years, increasing the demand for ever-taller structures in ever-denser cities. . . . [N]ew materials like CLT could make a huge difference in the Earth's health.

Source: Clay Risen. "Cross-Laminated Timber." *Popular Science*. Popular Science, February 26, 2014. Web. Accessed April 13, 2017.

Point of View

Take a close look at this passage. What does the writer say about CLT? How does he think building with CLT can affect the Earth?

FAST FACTS

- As of 2017, Dubai's Burj Khalifa is the world's tallest building at 2,717 feet (828 m).

- Burj Khalifa is a vertical city with residences, offices, shopping, and fitness facilities.

- Math, science, engineering, and computer technology were used to design and build Burj Khalifa.

- Burj Khalifa was built to withstand gravity and wind forces.

- Structural engineer William Baker developed the tower's buttressed core design.

- Vortex shedding occurs when wind patterns create suction around a tall building.

- Burj Khalifa's setbacks vary its shape and reduce the force of the wind.

- Burj Khalifa's foundation contains friction pilings, anchors it to the ground, and supports its massive weight.

- Jump form construction was used to build Burj Khalifa's superstructure.

- High-powered pumps were used to move concrete to upper floors.

- More than 24,000 glass panels make up Burj Khalifa's protective cladding.

- The building's cladding keeps out harmful rays from the sun and prevents overheating.

- Burj Khalifa's mechanical, electrical, and plumbing (MEP) system is located in its central core.

- All of Burj Khalifa's processes are controlled and monitored from a central computer room.

- Safety measures include fireproof concrete, fire-resistant building materials, exhaust systems, and refuge areas.

- Burj Khalifa is a popular tourist destination.

- By 2017, new skyscrapers taller than Burj Khalifa were planned or under construction.

STOP AND
THINK

Surprise Me

Chapter One discusses how plans were made to build Burj Khalifa. After reading this book, which two or three facts about the design of Burj Khalifa did you find most surprising? Write a few sentences about each fact. Why did you find each fact surprising?

Dig Deeper

After reading this book, what questions do you still have about Burj Khalifa? With an adult's help, find a few reliable sources that can help you answer your questions. Write a paragraph about what you learned.

Take a Stand

Some people believe supertall skyscrapers use up too much energy and other resources. Others say that living vertically in cities is more efficient. Tall cities can shelter more people on less land and reduce transportation needs. What is your opinion on the construction of mega-skyscrapers?

You Are There

This book discusses constructing Burj Khalifa. Imagine you live or work in Burj Khalifa. Write a journal entry describing what a day in your life is like. On what floor do you live or work? What is the view like from your room? How do you travel in the building? What activities do you do? Be sure to add plenty of detail to your description.

GLOSSARY

bedrock
a layer of solid rock beneath an area's loose soil

buttress
a member that projects outward and supports a wall

cladding
a covering

floor slab
wide, flat parts of a building that form the floors and ceilings

indigenous
original to a place

members
parts of a complex structure

mimic
to copy

spire
a structure at the top of a building that narrows to a point

stalactite
a rock formation that hangs from the ceiling of a cave

strike
a refusal to work in protest of poor pay, dangerous working conditions, or other reasons

vanity
having too much pride

ONLINE
RESOURCES

To learn more about Burj Khalifa, visit our free resource websites below.

Visit **abdocorelibrary.com** for free Common Core resources for teachers and students, including vetted activities, multimedia, and booklinks, for deeper subject comprehension.

Visit **abdobooklinks.com** for free additional online weblinks for further learning. These links are routinely monitored and updated to provide the most current information available.

LEARN
MORE

Cornille, Didier. *Skyscrapers*. New York: Princeton, 2014.

McCarthy, Cecilia Pinto. *Engineering One World Trade Center*. Minneapolis, MN: Abdo Publishing, 2017.

INDEX

About the Author

Cecilia Pinto McCarthy has written several nonfiction books for children. When she is not writing, she enjoys teaching ecology classes at a nature sanctuary. She lives with her family north of Boston, Massachusetts.

32 29   7/19 ①